AR:L-2.11p-0.5

Welcome to Kenya

by Alison Auch

Content and Reading Adviser: Mary Beth Fletcher, Ed.D.
Educational Consultant/Reading Specialist
The Carroll School, Lincoln, Massachusetts

Spyglass
BOOKS

COMPASS POINT BOOKS

Minneapolis, Minnesota

Compass Point Books
3722 West 50th Street, #115
Minneapolis, MN 55410

Visit Compass Point Books on the Internet at *www.compasspointbooks.com*
or e-mail your request to *custserv@compasspointbooks.com*

Photographs ©: Wolfgang Kaehler/Corbis, cover; PhotoDisc, cover (background), 10;
Buddy Mays/Corbis, 4; Corel, 6, 7, 8, 9, 11, 12, 13, 14, 15, 16, 17.

Project Manager: Rebecca Weber McEwen
Editor: Heidi Schoof
Photo Selectors: Rebecca Weber McEwen and Heidi Schoof
Designers: Jaime Martens and Les Tranby
Illustrator: Svetlana Zhurkina

Library of Congress Cataloging-in-Publication Data

Auch, Alison.
  Welcome to Kenya / by Alison Auch.
      v. cm. — (Spyglass books)
Includes bibliographical references and index.
Contents: Where is Kenya? — In the village — Many clothes, many people
— Spoon food — A baby is born! — "How elephants became wild."
  ISBN 0-7565-0369-8 (hardcover)
  1. Kenya—Social life and customs—Juvenile literature.
  [1. Kenya—Social life and customs.] I. Title. II. Series.
  DT433.54 .A93 2002
  967.62—dc21
                              2002002752

Contents

Where Is Kenya?

Welcome to my country!

I live in Kenya.

It is on the east coast of Africa.

I want to tell you about my beautiful home.

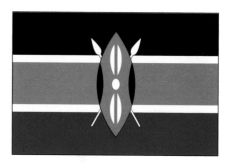

Kenyan Flag

Did You Know?

The *equator* runs through the middle of Kenya.

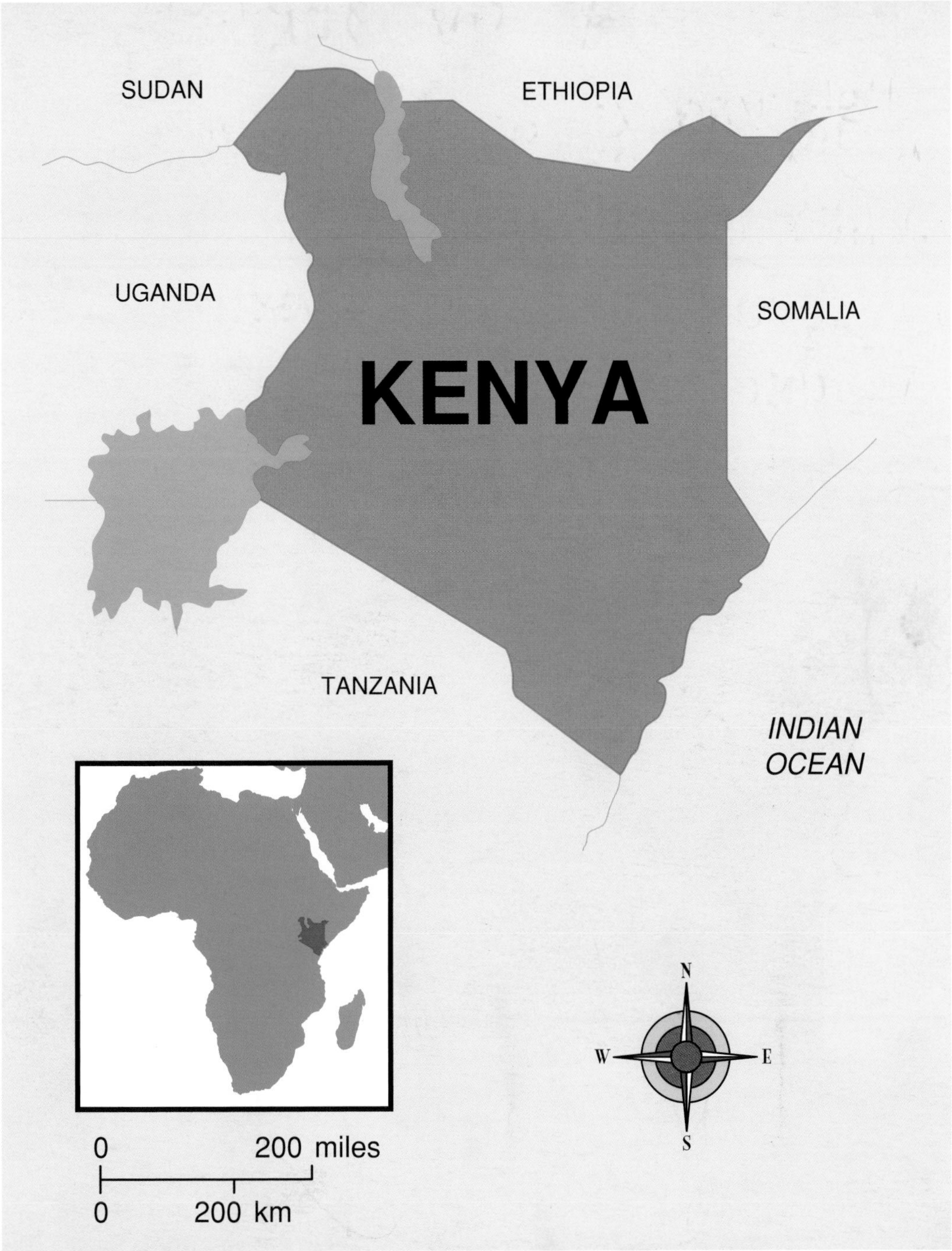

SUDAN

ETHIOPIA

UGANDA

SOMALIA

KENYA

TANZANIA

INDIAN
OCEAN

0   200 miles

0   200 km

N

W   E

S

At Home

My family lives in a farming village. Our home has grass mixed with mud on the roof. This keeps out the rain.

People who live in small towns often work together. They farm the rich land.

At Work

My father has a good job.
He takes *visitors* out in
a car. They look at
wild animals.

Many women work at
the town market.

Spoon Food

We like to eat ugali.
It is like thick oatmeal made
from corn. Many people grow
corn on their farms.

These water buffalo look like cattle, but they are very wild. Sometimes they break our fences and *trample* our *crops.*

Beautiful Clothes

In Kenya, many people wear the same kinds of clothes people wore long ago. We like clothes that keep us cool in the hot sun.

During dances and other ceremonies, some people wear fancy *headdresses.*

A Baby Is Born!

When a baby is born in our village, we are happy. We eat and dance all day long.

People dance to the beat of drums.

Fun Facts

Kenya is known for its wildlife. It has big cities, too!

Kenya has cheetahs, which are the fastest animals on Earth.

People in Kenya speak different *languages.* This girl may speak *Swahili,* English, and the language of her village.

After years of hunting, many animals in Kenya were *endangered.* Now there are big parks where these animals can live in safety.

How Elephants
Became Wild

Long ago, elephants
and people were friends.

One day, a woman asked
an elephant to bring her
some firewood from
the forest.

The elephant did not bring
much wood, but it was
the best wood.
The woman was mad. Why
didn't he bring more wood?

The elephant's feelings were hurt. He left the village. From that day on, people and elephants lived apart.

Index

GR: F
Word Count: 191

From Alison Auch

Reading and writing are my favorite things to do. When I'm not reading or writing, I like to go to the mountains or play with my little girl, Chloe.